THE MESSAGE

of

SAINT SERAPHIM

IRINA GORAINOV

SLG Press
Convent of the Incarnation Fairacres
Parker Street Oxford OX4 1TB England
www.slgpress.co.uk

The Message of Saint Seraphim

This impression 2013

ISBN 978-0-7283-0020-0
ISSN 0307-1405

Printed by:

Joshua Horgan Oxford England

FOREWORD

In the time of the Soviet Union, when Christians in Russia often lived in circumstances of extreme difficulty and at times of direct persecution, the words and example of St Seraphim were a living reality for people, bringing hope and new strength to those who could be tempted to despair. But the message itself, of course, was not for that time alone, nor for his own people alone, but for Christians of every nation and tradition, no less now than then.

In the communist time Sarov itself was a 'closed' city which it was virtually impossible to visit. The nearby Community of Diveyevo, which St Seraphim himself had so much helped and guided, was totally suppressed. Now it is again a flourishing centre of prayer and pilgrimage, a Community with more than four hundred Sisters. The relics of St Seraphim himself, which in the Soviet time had been hidden away in a basement in Leningrad, are now restored to the Community church, and pilgrims come from not only all over Russia but from across the world.

The word *staretz*, which often occurs in this account of St Seraphim, is simply the Russian for 'old man'; it is a title given to a monk in the Eastern Church, whether a layman or ordained, as was Father Seraphim, who has received from the Spirit the gifts of discernment, wisdom, counsel and healing. Irina Gorainov, who wrote this account of the message of St Seraphim, lived for some years on the island of Patmos and thus was privileged to know well one of the greatest of the *startzi* of modern Greece, Father Amphilochius, who died in the spring of 1971. What she has given us here, therefore, is based not only on her knowledge of the written sources of the life of St Seraphim, but on her personal acquaintance with men and women who were living in the same tradition of prayer and faith, the tradition which now flourishes again at Sarov itself.

The substance of this pamphlet was first given as a lecture at the annual conference of the Fellowship of St Alban and St Sergius in Liverpool in 1972. It was the immediate wish of those who heard it that the lecture should be made available to many others. The revelation of the presence of the Holy Spirit, given through the humble Seraphim, is, as he himself declared, intended for the whole world. At a time when Christian people in the many parts of the world, from China to South America for instance, are coming to new understanding and experience of the gifts of the Holy Spirit, the teaching of the *staretz* has a particular and startling relevance. The very aim of Christian life, he tells us, is to receive the Holy Spirit. 'The heart of man is capable of containing the Kingdom of God. The Holy Spirit and the Kingdom of God are one.'

A. M. ALLCHIN
November 2006

I

THE DISCOVERY OF A MANUSCRIPT

COVERED WITH DUST, pigeons' feathers and dung, a voluminous parcel, weighing several pounds, was entrusted to the writer Serge Nilus in 1902 as on his way from Sarov he stopped at the convent of Diveyevo, founded by the famous staretz Seraphim. The parcel, which for many years had lain forgotten in an attic, belonged to the widow of a rich landlord, Nicholas Motovilov, who in his youth had been cured by the staretz Seraphim from what was probably a hopeless case of quickly spreading general paralysis. Throughout his life (he outlived the staretz by many years) Motovilov would call himself Father Seraphim's 'devoted little servant'. He took an active part in the accomplishment of Father Seraphim's will, especially as far as his beloved convent of Diveyevo was concerned, and he married a niece of one of the nuns and left to her his notes and memoirs. A simple soul, she deposited them in the attic. Feeling, however, the approach of her own death, she decided to pass them on to someone who might be interested in reading them.

Nilus took the papers eagerly, but great was his disappointment when he started to sort them out. Most of them were bills, vouchers, copies of petitions concerning Motovilov's estates or old personal letters of no importance whatsoever. Worst of all, Nilus had the greatest difficulty in reading Motovilov's handwriting. Almost ready to give up, he desperately addressed himself one evening to the staretz Seraphim himself : 'Father' he cried, 'is it possible that you have made me find the papers of your "little servant" Motovilov in such an out of the way place as Diveyevo, only to let them fall back into oblivion again?' The next morning he discovered, in the heap of rubbish he had been handling, a copybook filled with Motovilov's handwriting which overnight he had acquired the capacity of deciphering. Moreover, his eyes fell upon the following sentence which Father Seraphim had pronounced: 'I am sure the Lord will help you to keep all these things in mind. Especially because the manifestation of his grace was not destined for you alone but, through your intervention, for the entire world.'

What grace? What manifestation? Was he a prophet, the humble staretz who, some seventy years in advance, could predict with such calm assurance the universal spreading of a message entrusted in the thickness of Russian woods to an insignificant young layman?

Nilus published the now famous conversation with Motovilov in the July issue of the *Moscow Journal* under the title: 'How the Spirit of God manifested itself in Saint Seraphim during his conversation concerning the aim of Christian life.' He could write 'Saint' Seraphim because precisely in July of that year 1903 the staretz had been officially canonised by the Orthodox Church.

A Conventional Monk

Prokhor Mochnin, later known as Seraphim of Sarov, was born in July 1759 in the town of Kursk on the northern outskirts of the Russian steppes. His father owned a brick factory and was known as a reliable building contractor. He was busy building a church when, at the age of forty, he died. It was his widow, an active, intelligent, charitable and devout woman who, after his death, finished building the church and brought up her two young sons. Prokhor was profoundly influenced by her and all his life remained devoted to her memory.

Tearing himself away from home, however, at the age of nineteen he entered a monastery situated in the midst of the immense forests which cover the centre of Russia (south of Nizhni-Novgorod and north of Tambov). Because of its remoteness from human habitation and the wilderness of the surrounding nature it was called a 'desert'—the Desert of Sarov. Prokhor was to remain within its walls until the age of thirty-five, first as a novice, then as a regular monk, given the name of Seraphim (in Hebrew, 'flaming'), finally as ordained deacon and priest. But the wilderness called him. He asked, and obtained, permission to retire to the woods, and became a real 'Desert Father'.

But let us cast a glance at those sixteen years during which the handsome, fair-haired, blue-eyed, broad-shouldered young man disciplined himself to become an exemplary conventional monk, obedient to his superiors, cheerfully accomplishing the various tasks assigned to him, singing in the choir, strictly following all monastic rules. Endowed with great physical strength, he loved to work outdoors with the brethren, cutting down trees and making rafts to float down the river. 'Physical work and reading of the Scriptures contribute toward keeping one's mind and body clean', he used to say, paraphrasing his favourite author, St Isaac the Syrian, a seventh century mystic. He was also fond of carpentry. He accompanied all his activities by the unceasing 'prayer of Jesus', hesychasm having made its way into Russian monasteries, as had also the *Philokalia,* translated into Russian.

Did he work too hard? He fell ill with dropsy. For three years he had been ailing, and finally his condition appeared to be hopeless. He refused doctors' help and asked only for Holy Communion. The Abbot, who loved him dearly, celebrated a liturgy. The monks prayed. To everybody's surprise the young man recovered almost immediately. A tradition relates that he had dozed off and, in a state of half waking, half sleeping, he saw the Queen of Heaven, the glorious Virgin Mary, enter his cell. She was accompanied by the Apostles, St John and St Peter. Turning towards them and pointing to the sufferer, she pronounced strange words: *'He is of our race.'* Then with a staff which she had in her hand, she touched the young monk's side, an opening appeared in it, and the water with which his body had been full flowed out. It is said that, as an old man, he showed the mark which remained on his side.

Appointed deacon, he served in church with ever-increasing zeal. Angels, Orthodoxy believes, concelebrate invisibly during the liturgy. Father Seraphim saw them. Once he was favoured with a vision of Christ himself entering the church accompanied by the heavenly hosts. He blessed the congregation and the deacon Seraphim in particular. For three hours Seraphim remained motionless as if struck by lightning. His superiors warned him severely against the danger of visions. The monks began to eye him suspiciously. Was Father Seraphim, the cheerful, reliable young fellow, the stalwart woodcutter, the intelligent, efficient workman, turning into a 'mystic'—something of which Orthodox monks are particularly suspicious?

However, Father Seraphim was no longer a novice in the spiritual realm. He knew full well that humility is the basis of all growth; he also knew that the closer one gets to God, the more, realizing one's unworthiness, one hungers for him. He asked permission to lead a hermit's life in the forest, and officially obtained it. Thus, at the age of thirty-five the first period of his monastic life ended.

The Hermit

His hermitage was a plain wooden *isba* (cabin) standing under giant pine trees on the steep bank of the little river Sarovka. Its furniture consisted of a table, a log for a chair, an icon in a corner—no bed.

What does a hermit do all day long? He prays. He works. Following the rule of Saint Pachomius established in the fourth century, Father Seraphim rose at midnight to start the day by singing matins. Canonical hours followed, then vespers and, before going to sleep, long evening prayers accompanied by numerous genuflexions and prostrations. Every day he read the Gospels—'A man's mind must swim in the holy scriptures', he said—and the forest resounded with his singing of psalms. He had a small vegetable garden, kept bees, and acted as a woodcutter.

In the desert a man becomes a cosmic figure. Confronted with the essential, he works at his own purification and transfiguration, at the same time contributing to the ultimate transfiguration of the world which, as Saint Paul says, bears the burden of human sin and awaits liberation.

Such is the hermit's task, and he does not labour in vain. Animals understand him. In Syria and Egypt the Fathers of the Desert had their friendly lions and hyenas. St Francis of Assisi had his falcon and his wolf. St Seraphim of Sarov, like St Sergius of Radonezh before him, had his bear who like a dog, lay at his feet and obeyed his commands. After he had finished his midnight prayers, Father Seraphim came out of his hut and was surrounded by the inhabitants of the forest, wolves, foxes, hares, lizards and snakes who had come for their first breakfast. 'How is it that you have bread enough in your bag for all of them?' an occasional eye-witness asked. 'There is always enough', replied the hermit.

But working thus, in peace and love, for universal transfiguration and sanctification, goes against the Devil's designs. Before starting his mission of the redemption of the human race, our Lord, in the desert, was confronted by the Enemy, and all the Fathers of the Desert have had to bear his assaults. Seraphim of Sarov was no exception.

It is not fashionable nowadays to believe in the Devil. 'Does he really exist?' Motovilov once asked the staretz. 'What do they teach you in your universities?' asked Seraphim quizzically. 'Of course he exists.' He spoke from experience.

At first the demons tried to frighten him out of the forest. Then they flooded his mind with doubts and blasphemous thoughts. 'Lord have mercy upon me!' cried Seraphim for a thousand nights and a thousand days, standing, like a stylite, on a flat stone outdoors, or in a cavity under his *isba*. The temptation vanished. But the evil forces prompted three peasants to look for money in the hermit's dwelling. Confronted with their arrogance, the staretz could have defended himself. Not yet fifty, he was in full possession of his great physical strength, and he had his hatchet in his hand. But he thought of Christ's non-resistance to evil and, dropping his hatchet and crossing his arms on his breast, calmly said, 'Do what you have come to do'. One of the ruffians picked up the hatchet and struck the hermit on the head. He fell down, unconscious, was kicked, beaten, bound and left for dead, while the would-be robbers ran into the cabin to look for the hidden treasure. All they found were a few potatoes in a corner and, suddenly terrified by what they had done, they fled. When later they were caught, Father Seraphim insisted that they should not be punished. The forgiveness of sins has always been, to Russians, the touchstone of true Christianity.

Meanwhile, carried back to the monastery, Father Seraphim seemed to be dying. He could neither sleep nor eat. The doctors, called to his bedside, diagnosed a broken skull, broken ribs, innumerable wounds and bruises. As they were gravely whispering among themselves, exchanging Latin terms, he closed his eyes and dozed off. Again, clad in her royal raiment, the glorious Mother of God entered his cell. And again she was accompanied by the Apostles Peter and John. Looking at the doctors she said: 'What of their efforts? *He is of our race.*' Seraphim opened his eyes—she had gone. Later, filled with energy and exaltation, he began to get up and, refusing the doctors' aid, took a few steps in his room. By the evening he was able to eat a little food.

Father Seraphim got well and, several months later, returned to the forest. He was no longer, however, the sturdy woodcutter known for his physical strength but, at under fifty, a broken old man, a cripple painfully limping along, leaning on a staff or on his hatchet.

Why did he insist, in spite of his superior's warning, on going back into the wilderness? Another ascetic feat lay in store for him: he entered into complete silence. To pray without words is the climax of hesychast prayer. 'The silence of the serene is prayer', wrote Isaac the Syrian, 'for his very thoughts are divine impulses. The motions of the pure mind are quiet voices, secretly chanting psalms to him who is invisible.'[1] The Holy Ghost is in possession of such a man. It is he who prays in the silence of his heart.

Father Seraphim even stopped going to the monastery on Sundays as he had been wont to do, incurring the wrath of the new Abbot—a spiritual stranger—and scandalizing the monks. An ultimatum was sent to him: attend the liturgy every Sunday or, if his sick legs did not permit him to walk the six kilometres separating the hermitage from the monastery, return to live within its walls.

The staretz Seraphim had developed into a quite unconventional monk. Instead of wearing black, he dressed in white. On his feet, like a peasant, he wore *lapti* made of birch's bark. He evaded all encounters, and when by chance he met someone in the forest, fell down upon his face and remained in that position until the stranger had gone. But he remained an obedient son of the Church. Obedience, for a monk, is the first of all virtues, Seraphim himself taught. And he acted accordingly.

Leaving his dear forest hermitage where for years he had lived, meditated and prayed, he returned to the monastery and shut himself up in his cell. His period of silence was not over. For five years, from 1810 to 1815, he remained a voluntary prisoner in his cell, a dingy place with a coffin hewn out of a tree trunk at the entrance. Not even the monk who once a day brought him his food—a bit of sauerkraut and a bowl of dry oatmeal—could see his face, for he covered it with a towel.

[1] *Mystic Treatises of Isaac of Nineveh,* trans. A. J. Wensinck, Amsterdam, 1923, p. 174 (trans. directly from the Syriac); an alternative version in English (via the Greek) is to be found in the *Ascetical Homilies of St Isaac the Syrian*, The Holy Transfiguration Monastery, Boston, 1984, p. 182.

What did he do? He read the gospels (Matthew on Monday, Mark on Tuesday, and so on), prayed, and had visions. Once, like St Paul, he was caught up into heaven to see the dwellings God prepares for those who love him. But terrible headaches due to lack of exercise and fresh air compelled him to pray for liberation. The Virgin Mary appeared to him in his sleep and bade him return to the forest.

The Staretz

No sooner did the rumour spread that Father Seraphim had left his cell than people eager to see him flocked to Sarov. 'So many people come to visit Father Seraphim', the Abbot said angrily, 'that we cannot shut the monastery gate until midnight'.

What did they see? A little old man clad in white, all dried up, with fine, severe features and kind blue eyes. His smile was like that of a child. He met his visitors gaily, calling them 'My joy', and often adding the Easter greeting, 'Christ is risen!'

From his youth he had lived in the monastery, then in the hermitage in the woods, finally as a recluse in his narrow cell. Life had rolled past him with its changes of rulers, revolutions, wars. Napoleon had invaded Russia. Was he aware of it? People said his prayers had saved the country.

What was it in him that attracted the crowds which in ever increasing numbers flocked to Sarov? What had he learned in his seclusion that could be useful to people painfully struggling in the world? He himself tells us, when he says:

Have peace in your heart,
and thousands around you will be saved.

Having conquered his flesh, and having been filled with the Spirit, the staretz Seraphim radiated precisely those fruits of the Spirit, love, joy, peace, of which St Paul speaks (Gal. 5: 22) and which people of all times and of all classes of society are in such dire need, and which no earthly goods, no social improvements, no psychiatrists can give.

He read peoples' thoughts, predicted their future, gently showed them their way in life, healed their spiritual as well as their physical ailments. Despair he termed the greatest of sins, the substitution of fear for mercy—the annihilation of Christianity. He never 'preached'. He was himself a living example, a living symbol. 'It is easy to make beautiful sermons', he said with that mixture of good-natured humour, humility and inflexible authority which was his, 'just as easy as to throw stones from the top of our belfry. But to live what one preaches is as difficult as to carry stones to the top of the belfry.'

II

THE MESSAGE

IT IS TO THIS MAN, whose reputation had already spread to the furthest corners of European and Asiatic Russia, that a young landlord, Nicolas Motovilov, addressed himself in the hope of being healed from a quickly spreading paralysis. In his memoirs we read the detailed and vivid account of how, after having confessed his faith in Jesus Christ and his Holy Mother, he was almost instantly made whole. This happened in September 1831. Motovilov often returned to see his benefactor and in November of the same year had an important conversation with the staretz, thirteen months before the latter's death, which he recorded and which was what Nilus discovered among the papers and published seventy-two years later.

Typical of St Seraphim is the fact that the conversation—like the healing that preceded it—took place in the open, under an old pine tree on the bank of the river Sarovka. 'It was on a Thursday', Motovilov writes, 'the sky was grey, the ground was covered with several inches of snow.' And it was snowing—snowing slowly, leisurely, the way it often does in Russia. Nevertheless the staretz bade his young friend sit on the trunk of a fallen tree and himself squatted in front of him.

'The Lord has revealed to me', he said, 'that, from childhood on you have been desirous to know in what the real aim of Christian life consists.' This was true. But Motovilov had never yet spoken to the staretz about it. 'You put the question to many people, even to ecclesiastical dignitaries, but never received a satisfactory answer. You were told that you should go to church, behave according to Christ's commandments, be charitable, etc. Some even disapproved of what they called your misplaced curiosity. They were wrong. As for me, the humble Seraphim, I'll tell you in what that aim really consists: The aim of Christian life is the acquisition of the Holy Spirit.'

Motovilov was surprised. 'The Holy Spirit?'

The Holy Spirit, the Third Person of the Trinity who, after Christ's ascension and glorification, came down to give life to the Church, the mystical body of the Son; who had guided the Apostles; whom the Greek Fathers exalted and the mystics saw as light. The reality of his presence, of his mysterious self-giving personality, had so faded, not only among Westerns but in the Christian East, that in the nineteenth century, the thought of him had ceased to play a part in the average layman's life.

'Prayer, fasting, good deeds accomplished in the name of Christ', the staretz went on, 'commendable as they are, cannot be considered as aims. They are means, earthly goods with which one must trade in order to put the benefits obtained in the savings bank of the Spirit.'

In a very original way the staretz proceeded to interpret the parable of the Ten Virgins:

> Some think that the lack of oil in the Foolish Virgins' lamps corresponds to a lack of virtuous deeds during their lifetime. This is not entirely correct. They did not lack virtue—for were they not virgins? What they lacked was the Holy Spirit. They did not seek him. They accomplished good deeds and believed in them. But good deeds in themselves are nothing. If not done in the name of Christ, but out of vanity or for one's own satisfaction, they may even turn into evil. What contributes to our salvation is not virtuous actions, or their quantity, but the fruit which they bear—the grace of the Holy Spirit. Because by abiding in us the Holy Spirit, the Third Person of the Trinity, prepares our soul and body to be the seat, the throne of the Trinity itself, in accordance with God's promise to 'come and dwell' in us.

St Seraphim meant that the Holy Spirit is the agent of our deification, in accordance with the Orthodox way of reading the Scriptures and the patristic saying: 'Man is a creature who has received the order to become god.'

Sacramentally, the Holy Spirit has always been symbolized by oil.

The staretz continued:

> The oil the Wise Virgins had in their lamps permitted them to wait for the arrival of the Bridegroom and to enter with him into the chamber of eternal joy. As to the foolish ones, they had to go to the market. The market symbolizes our life; the closed door of the chamber—our death. As to the oil, it represents the grace by which the Holy Spirit, filling our being, transforms—transfigures—the corruptible into the incorruptible, physical death into spiritual life, the stable in which our passions are chained like beasts into a temple of God, a nuptial chamber where we are to meet our Lord and Saviour, Bridegroom of our souls.'

Prayer

The saint went on to talk about prayer which, as he believed, more than anything else, gives us the grace of the Holy Spirit, and which is always at our disposal, wherever we are, whatever we do.

'You consider it a privilege to speak with the humble Seraphim', he said to Motovilov, 'persuaded as you are that he is not devoid of grace. How about conversing with God himself?'

Here the staretz said an unusual thing.

> One must pray, however, only until the Holy Spirit descends upon us and gives us, in a measure known to him alone, his celestial grace. Visited by him, we must stop praying. Why indeed go on imploring him: 'Come, make thy dwelling in us, cleanse us from all evil and save us by thy goodness' [words from an Orthodox prayer], when he has already come? Suppose you have invited me to your house, and I have arrived. But you continue to invite me repeating, 'Please come!' I would certainly think: 'He has gone out of his mind. I am here, and yet he continues to invite me!' So when the Holy Ghost deigns to visit us we must stop praying, uttering words. The soul must be

> absolutely silent in order to hear and understand his message.

Action

Impatient of prayer, as we all are, Motovilov asked how one might acquire the Holy Spirit by other means. 'By trading with any action which gives us the benefit of his grace', the staretz answered. His teaching exactly accords with that of St Paul in the First Letter to the Corinthians where the Apostle says:

> Now there are diversities of gifts, but the same Spirit. And there are differences of administrations, but the same Lord. And there are diversities of operations, but it is the same God which worketh all in all. But the manifestation of the Spirit is given to every man to profit withal (I Cor. 12: 4-7).

And the staretz added:

> Trade with your spiritual virtues. Distribute the gifts of grace to whoever asks for them. A burning candle lights other candles without losing its own brilliance. Earthly riches, when distributed, diminish. But heavenly riches, when distributed, increase.

Can One See God?

'Father' said Motovilov, 'you speak of the acquisition of the Holy Spirit as being the aim of Christian life, but how can I recognize him? Actions are visible. But the Holy Spirit is not. How can I know whether I am in possession of him?'

Without knowing it, Motovilov had put a theological question of the utmost importance. It had been raised many times. Eastern Orthodox mystics have always replied in the affirmative—that we can know the presence of God within. They saw divinity as 'uncreated' light.

'God is light', wrote Symeon the New Theologian, Abbot of the monastery of St Mamas in Constantinople, at the beginning of the eleventh century. And the saint continued,

> He communicates his brilliance to those who unite themselves with him, in the measure of their purification. Man unites himself to God spiritually and bodily, because his soul is not separated from his spirit, nor his body from his soul. God enters into communication with man as a whole.[2]

> The One who is God by nature converses with those he made gods by grace. ... The Holy Spirit in them becomes all the Scriptures tell us about the Kingdom of God ...[3]

'The Holy Spirit is Light' said the staretz Seraphim to Motovilov. But Motovilov did not seem to be satisfied. 'I want to understand it better ...'

The Transfiguration

'My friend, we are both at this moment in the Spirit of God. Why won't you look at me?'

'I can't look at you, Father', Motovilov replied, 'your eyes shine like lightning; your face has become more dazzling than the sun, and it hurts my eyes to look at you'.

'Don't be afraid' he said, 'at this very moment you've become as bright as I have. You are also at present in the fullness of the Spirit of God; otherwise you wouldn't be able to see me as you do see me.'

And leaning towards him he whispered in his ear:

> Thank the Lord for his infinite goodness towards us. As you've noticed, I haven't even made the sign of the cross; it was quite enough that I had prayed to God in my thoughts, in my heart, saying within myself: 'Lord, make him worthy to see clearly with his bodily eyes, the descent of your Spirit, with which you favour your servants when you condescend to appear to them in the wonderful radiance of your glory.' And, as you see my friend, the Lord at once granted this prayer of the humble Seraphim ... How thankful we ought to be to God for this unspeakable gift

[2] Russian Edition of 'Mount Athos' I, Sermon 25, p. 228.
[3] Ibid. II, Sermon 90, pp. 788-789.

> which he has granted us both. Even the Fathers of the Desert did not always have such manifestations of his goodness. The grace of God, like a mother full of loving kindness towards her children, has deigned to comfort your afflicted heart, at the intercession of the Mother of God herself … Why then, my friend, do you not look me straight in the face? Look freely and without fear; the Lord is with us.

Motovilov's account goes on: 'Encouraged by these words, I looked and was seized by holy fear. Imagine in the middle of the sun, dazzling in the brilliance of its noontide rays, the face of the man who is speaking to you. You can see the movements of his lips, the changing expression of his eyes, you can hear his voice, you can feel his hands holding you by the shoulders, but you can see neither his hands nor his body—nothing except the blaze of light which shines around, lighting up with its brilliance the snow-covered meadow, and the snowflakes which continue to fall unceasingly.'

'What do you feel?' asked Father Seraphim.

'An immeasurable well-being' I replied.

'But what sort of well-being? What exactly?'

'I feel', I replied, 'such calm, such peace in my soul, that I can find no words to express it.'

'My friend, it is the peace our Lord spoke of when he said to his disciples: "My peace I give unto you ", the peace which the world cannot give, "the peace which passes all understanding". What else do you feel?'

'Infinite joy in my heart.'

Father Seraphim continued:

> When the Spirit of God descends on a man, and envelops him in the fullness of his presence, the soul overflows with unspeakable joy, for the Holy Spirit fills everything he touches with joy … If the first-fruits of future joy have already filled your soul with such sweetness, with such happiness, what shall we say of the joy in the Kingdom of Heaven, which awaits all those who weep here on earth.

> You also, my friend, have wept during your earthly life, but see the joy which our Lord sends to console you here below. For the present we must work, and make continual efforts to gain more and more strength to attain 'the perfect measure of the stature of Christ ...' Then this transitory and partial joy which we now feel will be revealed in all its fullness, overwhelming our being with ineffable delights which no one will be able to take from us.

Saint Seraphim's Last Instructions to Motovilov

'From now on, you won't question me any more as to how the Holy Spirit visibly manifests himself', the staretz said. 'Will this manifestation always remain in your memory?' Motovilov replied that he feared his unworthiness would prevent him from remembering everything correctly. 'I feel sure', the staretz said, 'that God will help you to keep everything forever in your mind. Otherwise he would not have responded so rapidly to the humble Seraphim's prayer. Especially because the manifestation of the Holy Spirit was not meant for you alone, but for the entire world through your intervention. Strengthened in your faith, you will prove useful to others.'

The last instructions given by Father Seraphim to Motovilov are of a practical character.

> Remember that the Lord did not come down to earth to be served but to serve and to give life to a multitude. Act accordingly. Communicate the grace which you have experienced to any man desirous of salvation. Don't bury the silver which has been entrusted to you like the lazy servant did ... Nothing is impossible to one who believes. Ask, and your requests will be answered—provided that what you pray for is for the glory of God and the benefit of your brethren. You may formulate personal wishes, too; but be careful not to ask for things which you could easily have gone without. Yet do not think that a certain enjoyment of earthly goods is forbidden. The Lord knows we need them in order to make the difficult road we tread easier for us. He does not separate our welfare from his

glory ... He wants us to bear each other's burdens. Whatever one does to the least of his brethren one does to him.

The fact that I am a monk and you are a layman is of no importance.[4] The Lord listens equally to the monk and to the man of the world provided both are true believers. He looks for a heart full of true faith into which to send his Spirit. For the heart of a man is capable of containing the Kingdom of God. The Holy Spirit and the Kingdom of God are one.

'I have now told you everything' the staretz concluded. 'Go in peace. May the Lord and his Holy Mother be with you always. Amen.'

'During our conversation' added Motovilov, 'from the moment when Father Seraphim's face was illuminated, the vision of the light never ceased. I saw its extraordinary brilliance with my own eyes and am ready to certify to it under oath.'

Conclusion

Saint Seraphim, the servant of the Holy Spirit, was certainly a prophet. A prophet's vocation is double: not only does he foresee and predict the future, he also proclaims, sometimes incarnates, the truth.

From all that the saint said during his lifetime, it is clear that the approaching tragedy of his country had been revealed to him: the Revolution, the religious persecutions, the participation in the world wars. 'Life will be short then', he sighed with tears in his eyes. 'The Angels will hardly have time to gather up the souls.'

The publication of his posthumous message seems to have been timed to reach a world in particular need of the Comforter, and conscious of its need. A world suddenly

[4] Symeon the New Theologian had said the same thing in the eleventh century, but in the nineteenth century, it was quite an unusual statement to make!

broadened to cosmic dimensions, aspiring for universal unity, anxious for the Spirit of Truth, but at the same time a restless, uncertain, joyless and fearful world.

Can we see God as uncreated light? It seems doubtful, but we can all open ourselves to the grace of the Paraclete by removing obstacles to his coming: lukewarmness, self-sufficiency, intellectual pride, estrangement from Christianity and inattention which, according to the staretz, prevents us from reading and understanding the Scriptures correctly.

When asked if present day Christians lacked any of the conditions necessary to produce the same fruits of sanctity which had been so abundant in the past, the staretz replied: 'There is only one condition lacking—a firm resolve. *Jesus Christ is the same yesterday and today and forever.*'

About the Church and Brotherhood of St Seraphim, Little Walsingham, Norfolk

The icon on the cover of this book was painted by the Brotherhood of St Seraphim, based at the Orthodox church in Little Walsingham, and is reproduced with their permission and co-operation.

The Brotherhood of Saint Seraphim began on 8 December 1966, when the two founding members, who had spent the previous year in India with Archimandrite Lazarus Moore, were blessed by Archbishop Nikodim. The Archbishop sent them to Walsingham in response to a request made by the then Administrator of the Anglican Shrine, Canon Colin Stephenson, for someone to look after the little Orthodox chapel within the Anglican shrine and to be an Orthodox presence in the surrounding countryside. On arrival, they discovered that the only property they could afford to rent locally was the former railway station in Little Walsingham. Using this as their base, they set out to preach the Gospel in their daily contacts, in the services in the church, through icon painting—which was and remains a vital source of income—through printing liturgical texts, using translations made by Archimandrite Lazarus, and by helping those less fortunate than themselves.

All who came were welcomed; people of Russian, Greek and Cypriot origin, as well as British converts, joined together to honour the Mother of God in that place of pilgrimage. Bishops and priests came to serve the liturgy, both in the railway station chapel and in the Anglican shrine. Bishop Christophoros of Telmissos led annual visits from London each May, and these continued into the 1990s.

By 1978, the Brotherhood had come under the care of Metropolitan Anthony of Sourozh. Its priest, Father Mark, became a monk, taking the name of David, and he was joined by Mother Serafima. The church was now part of a monastery. Archimandrite David died in 1993.

This tiny church continues to be a place of mission and pilgrimage and to provide an ecumenical presence for a church with the Archdiocese of Orthodox Parishes of Russian Tradition in Western Europe, with a small monastic presence. Many Orthodox people have found it a place where, in the spirit of Saint Seraphim, they have been helped to know what they should do in their lives. It has provided a first experience of the Christian faith for many pilgrims and tourists, and a substantial number of people have found their way there into the Orthodox Church.

There is an icon-painting studio, where from the beginning icons have been painted in the traditional manner, and a small shop which caters for the needs of pilgrims selling icons, cards (including cards of many of the icons painted at St Seraphim's over the years), chotki, incense and booklets (including this one).

For many years, the church was privately rented by two local people who sustained its work from their own resources. More recently, an appeal has been made and the church is to be purchased by the St Seraphim's Trust.

Donations for this work are welcomed by:

St Seraphim's Trust, St Seraphim's Orthodox Church,
Station Road, Little Walsingham, Norfolk, NR22 6EB.

Cheques should be made payable to:

St Seraphim's Trust